PART 1

Walks from the Welsh Highland Railway

Part 1
Caernarfon to Rhyd-ddu

By Dave Salter
and Dave Worrall

First edition: 2003
Revised edition: 2009
© Text: Dave Salter/Dave Worrall

ISBN: 978-1-84524-117-9

First published in 2003 by Gwasg Carreg Gwalch

Revised edition published in 2009 by Llygad Gwalch,
Ysgubor Plas, Llwyndyrys, Pwllheli, Gwynedd LL53 6NG
☎ 01758 750432   📠 01758 750438
✆ books@carreg-gwalch.com
Web site: www.carreg-gwalch.com

Dedicated with admiration,
to the slatequarrymen of Gwynedd:
skilful in their work;
fervent for their culture;
fearless for their rights;
tender in their care for each other.

Some thoughts on the
Welsh Highland Railway

The re-opening of the Welsh Highland Railway has been a great welcome. Not only do we enjoy the sight of the trains and the sense of history associated with it but we recognise its potential. Of course, the tourists will enjoy seeing the magnificent Welsh countryside from these trains and hopefully local businesses will benefit from the increased trade. From our own point of view, it also brings a potential for some great walks using the trains and stations to link the starts and finishes.

We are not the only people to have used this form of transport for their inspiration; indeed we follow in the footsteps of two famous walkers. Showell Styles wrote the excellent *Walks from the Ffestiniog Railway*, and the great A Wainwright with his *Walks from Ratty*, which described a series of walks from the Ravenglass and Eskdale Railway. We could not hope to compete with these two greats, particularly the illustrations and maps of AW. However, our aim was quite simple, to provide the walker and tourist with the opportunity to see the countryside in a little more detail and at a more leisurely pace. Hopefully, a little of the history and character of the landscape will be absorbed before the train completes a memorable day in the Snowdonia countryside.

The Nant y Betws, is one of the quieter valleys and certainly when we were planning the walks we saw few people. The paths are certainly not as well trod as those in the Ogwen Valley and Llanberis area, but they deserve to be as well known. In a few years time those quiet paths may turn into deep tracks and the sense of solitude will be lost. So don't be put off, the walking from the Welsh Highland Railway will rival any of the paths found in the rest of Eryri *(Snowdonia)*. It is up to you to choose how high and how far you go. We have tried to include walks catering for everybody, so don't just ride the train there and back, get off the train, stretch your legs and take a walk.

We have found it beneficial to begin the day's activities by parking at the station where your walk will end. Then take the train to your start point and avoid the need to try and rush the walk in order to catch a train at the end of the day. Information about the times of the trains is available from the various stations or can be obtained by telephoning 01766 512340. Alternatively the website is a host of information, and at the time of writing was www.bangor.ac.uk/ml/whr/.

The enjoyment of each walk is dependant on being correctly equipped for the environment. The weather in Eryri can change rapidly and we would advise that good footwear and spare clothing would ensure that you are not caught out by the elements. There is nothing worse than finishing a walk cold, wet and miserable. Similarly, we have always believed that our books are guides and should not be considered as substitutes for the Ordnance Survey maps. Always take a map and compass with you and know how to use them. Being prepared for any walk will increase your chances of enjoying it and at the end of the day our hope is that you enjoy these walks.

Dave Salter and Dave Worrall

Contents

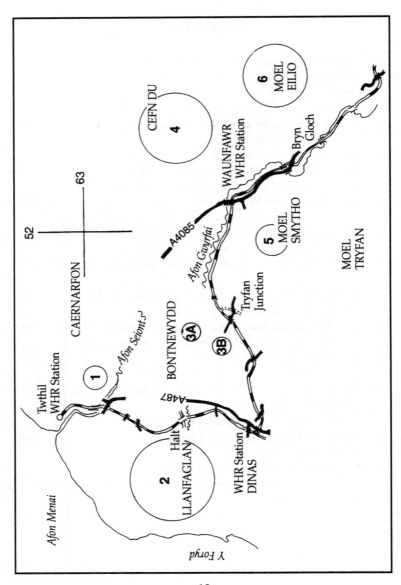

Caernarfon, Afon Seiont and Twthill

Maps: 1:50,000 sheet 115 Landranger Yr Wyddfa *(Snowdon)* and Caernarfon or 1:25,000 Outdoor Leisure sheet 17 Yr Wyddfa *(Snowdon)* and Conwy.
Distance: 4 Miles / 6.4 Kilometres.
Height gained: 147ft / 45 metres.
Duration: 2 Hours.
Terrain: Urban footpaths.
Stations/Halts: Caernarfon Station.
Car Park: Located on the Old Quay. Parking behind the Safeway store and by the Marina at Victoria Dock. G.R.481632.

Caernarfon has a fascinating history covering an astonishing period of time. On the walk, glimpses will be seen of that history and it is hoped that your own interest will encourage you to investigate further the rich detail of Caernarfon's past.

The first period of note began with the setting up of a Roman Military station. Segontium as it was called, was founded in AD 50 during the reign of Emperor Claudius by Ostorius Scapula. It was the terminus to the Roman road which ran from Chester *(Deva)* along the Welsh coast and helped establish Segontium as the chief Roman fortress in north western Wales. It was the main barracks for the Roman Legion during the period when they were invading Anglesey. In AD 61, they invaded under the command of Suetonius Paulinus, in AD 75 under Julius Frontius and later Agricola. Anglesey proved to be a difficult conquest for the Romans. In later years, AD 120, due to the work being carried out on Hadrians Wall and the subsequent invasion of Scotland in AD 140, the garrison at Segontium was greatly reduced. However, the threat of invasion from the Irish meant it had to be re-garrisoned. The fort was eventually evacuated for the last time around AD 300 when the Romans began to retire from northern Wales. The site of Segontium is half a mile from the present town centre on the road to Beddgelert. It occupies a

5 acre site of low level remains. The museum contains pottery and weapons from the Roman era and its displays will further explain the history of the Romans in the area.

The most imposing feature in Caernarfon is the remains of the Castle rising above the mouth of Afon Seiont. The construction of the castle commenced in 1283 under the direction of Henry de Elerton, with the town walls and towers being constructed by James of St George d'Esperanche. Both receiving their orders from Edward I, the castle took 40 years to complete. The castle was intended as the strongest link in a defensive chain, which Edward 1st called the Iron Ring. This was a string of fortresses built along the northern Wales coast, each fortress being a day's march from one another in order to be able to suppress the power of the Welsh Princes. It was at Caernarfon that Edward's son was born and to rub salt into the wounds of the Welsh people he declared the infant 'Prince of Wales', laying the foundations of a long tradition of mis-use of the title!

During its history, a number of attempts were made to destroy the castle, but only the attack by Prince Madog in 1294, when the walls were incomplete had any success. In 1646, the castle was captured by the Parliamentarians under General Mytton. Fortunately a government order to destroy it was not carried out. In 1969, and with much pomp and ceremony the young Prince Charles from Windsor was invested within the castle walls.

History now brings us to a period when Caernarfon owed its prosperity to the great slate industry. On the banks of Afon Seiont and further around the castle walls are the remains of slate quays. They now provide car parks and a thriving marina for pleasure craft. In the 1700's a very different type of vessel could be found tied up at the quayside. In 1730 alone, 101 vessels each carrying an average load of 16 tons of slate for export left these quays. They carried slate to Ireland and other ports around the coast of Britain. This traffic increased in the late 1700's to 237 vessels each carrying 35 tons of slate. Whilst the slate was being exported the ships imported goods such as gunpowder, flour and fertiliser. The town also provided many services for the boats and sailors. The Black Boy Inn is found on Stryd Pedwar a Chwech. This translates as four and six street, which in old shillings and pence was what sailors reputedly had to pay for a room, a bottle of spirits and a woman for the night. Northgate Street was the 'red light area' of the town. Apart from this sort of service industry, there was also a growth in engineering and ship repair works to support the slate trade. The original method of transporting the slate to Caernarfon from the quarries was pack horse or horse and cart. Then as quarries amalgamated railway links were established into the town. In 1828, the Nantlle Railway Company established a tramroad from the copper mines and slate quarries of Nantlle to the village of Penygroes and then on to the quays in Caernarfon. Early 1863 saw the owners of the various Llanberis slate quarries approach the L&NWR for a branch line from Caernarfon to Llanberis. In 1881 and unfortunately at the start of the decline of the slate industry, the North Wales Narrow Gauge Railway, carrying slate from the Quarries in Cwm Gwyrfai, opened. This line was the beginning of what was to become the Welsh Highland Railway. Its full history can be discovered in other publications and it is not the intention to cover it in any detail here when better accounts exist.

Caernarfon started to experience the unfortunate decline of the slate industry in 1870. This was mostly due to the high cost of transportation and also the introduction of new products to replace slate such as tiles, asbestos and ceramics. Many quarries closed in the early 1900's, re-opening again after the 1st World War when modern machinery helped improve production. However, decline continued up until the 1960's when the prospect of better working conditions and wages finally put an end to this hard, out of date existence that was the quarryman's lot.

The Walk: Descend from car park and follow dock wall around,

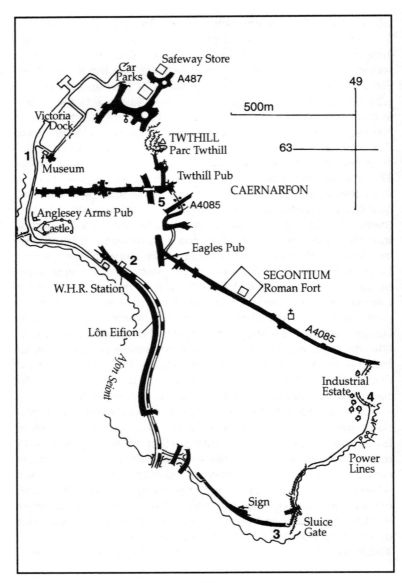

passing close to pay and display car park with Marina on R. Cross the rolling bridge over slipway. At end of dock (Victoria Dock) go R, passing museum on L and continue on to sea wall. **1.** L along sea wall passing the Anglesey Arms public house on L. Continue along the edge of the quay with the river on R, to end of carpark and storage shed (Caernarfon Harbour Trust Buoy Storage). Here L to small roundabout. **2.** R passing the Caernarfon Terminus of the Welsh Highland Railway and then half L on to and along Lôn Eifion cycle way. After passing under road bridge go L over railway line. R down path passing under new road bridge, at fork R, now following river. Half R along road passing sign for Hanson works on L. **3.** At very end of road L, with fence on L and path now runs with stream on R, later passing sluice gate. Under low bridge and up steps, R passing between brick pillars with Afon Seiont now on R. Continue on across open area passing close to power lines until a kissing gate is reached. **4.** Path now continues with fence and industrial site on R up to main road (A4085). L up road passing Cemetery on L and Church with tower on R. Continue down Constantine Road passing the site of Segontium on R. Cross over road junction and down to subway sign (The Eagles public house on opposite side of road). Continue along pavement over subway to road. L down minor road and then up to pelican crossing. **5.** Cross main road (A4086) and continue on up footpath. Cross next road at junction and pass 'Y Twthill' public house on R. Up Thomas street and over next road junction 'Twthill East'. Up lane passing sign Parc Twthill and up to view point. Retrace steps to 'Y Twthill' public house and R passing over footbridge. Down road to cross main road and continue under arches to return to sea wall. R to return to carparks.

Refreshments: The Black Boy Inn in Stryd Pedwar a Chwech *(Northgate Street)* does good food and has an interesting history but to be honest there is no shortage of eating establishments in Caernarfon.

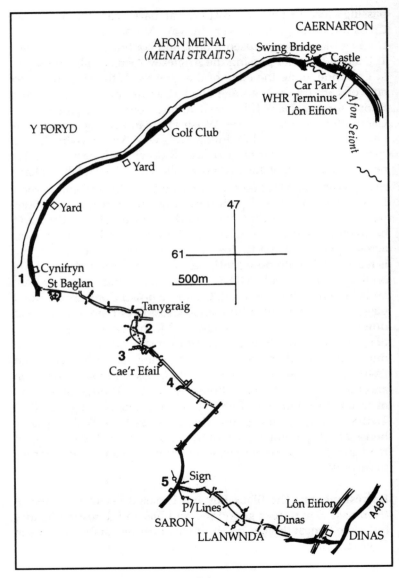

CAERNARFON

AFON MENAI
(MENAI STRAITS)

Swing Bridge

Castle

Car Park
WHR Terminus
Lôn Eifion

Afon Seiont

Y FORYD

Golf Club

Yard

Yard

47

61

500m

1 Cynifryn
St Baglan

Tanygraig

2

3
Cae'r Efail

4

5 Sign

P/Lines

SARON

LLANWNDA

Lôn Eifion
Dinas

A487

DINAS

Foryd to Dinas

Maps: 1:50,000 Landranger sheet 115 Yr Wyddfa *(Snowdon)* and Caernarfon or 1:25,000 Explorer sheet 13 Llŷn Peninsular East.
Distance: 4.5 miles/7.2 kilometres (allow an extra 3 miles/4.8 kilometres to return to Caernarfon via Lôn Eifion).
Height gained: 200ft/60metres.
Duration: 3 hours (allow extra 1.5 hours to return to Caernarfon by Lôn Eifion).
Terrain: Good underfoot on minor roads and Lôn Eifion itself, but can be wet across agricultural land.
Station/Halts: Caernarfon Station and Dinas Junction.
Car Park: If you are catching the train from Dinas to Caernarfon park in the Dinas Station car park at G.R.476586. If you are starting in Caernarfon a pay and display car park exists at the terminus of the Welsh Highland Railway at G.R.480626. To locate car park, on entering Caernarfon from either direction follow signs for the town centre/castle. Once in the centre (Y Maes/*Castle Square*), drive around the square in a clockwise direction heading towards the castle. Turn L towards the Quay car park and L just before it. Along the road for 150 metres passing small roundabout then L into the railway terminus car park. Other car parks exist in the town if you are not going to use the railway.

This excursion enables the walker to either treat the outing as a circular walk, by returning from Dinas by means of the gradually descending Lôn Eifion back into Caernarfon or to experience the joy of a nostalgic train journey into the town.

The walk departs from the historic town of Caernarfon passing over the swing bridge across Afon Seiont and following the coast road around the shoreline of Afon Menai. The walk heads towards the western end of the Afon Menai and the Foryd where on the Anglesey shore the peninsula of Abermenai point can be seen. Here the remains of a white building may be identified, and this marks the site of a once thriving ferry service. This service allowed travellers from Morfa Dinlle to visit Anglesey and those passengers from Niwbwrch *(Newborough)* and surrounding areas to visit the market in Caernarfon. This was one of the oldest ferries in the Afon Menai with reference being made to its existence as long ago as 1296.

On the Caernarfon promontory, opposite Abermenai and known as Morfa Dinlle, can be seen the structure of Fort Belan. This fort was constructed and garrisoned by the 1st Baron of Newborough in the late 18th Century. It was built to resist the threat of imminent invasion from the French during the Napoleonic wars. A few years after its initial construction a small dock was added by the 3rd Baron of Newborough to enable him to unload stone to reconstruct the family home, Glynllifon, which was destroyed by fire in 1836. In fact the family occupied the fort for 3 years during the reconstruction.

History has a habit of repeating itself and in 1940 when the shores of Britain were again threatened by invasion, the little fortress stood to arms and the resounding tramp of men and sentries keeping a keen vigil on the swirling tides of Afon Menai filled the small fort.

The fort later became a summer residence of Lord Newborough, who operated tours around it. Unfortunately for those inquisitive enough to wish to visit, the fort is now used only as holiday homes and access is restricted.

Headlines in a tabloid of 29th October 1998 drew attention to 'Peer to Eternity, wacky Aristocrats ashes fired from antique canon', and refers to Lord Newborough and the instructions he gave regarding his final resting place. He was a war hero and a veteran practical joker and on passing away, his family found a rather strange request in his will. His ashes were to be placed in a special container, fired from an antique canon and he was to be interred where they fell.

The late Lord had a distinguished war record, sailing into Dunkirk no fewer than 5 times to rescue troops. In 1942, he gained the DSC for the attempted destruction of the submarine pens at St Nazaire. Unfortunately losing an eye in the raid he was captured and incarcerated in Colditz, only to escape by faking madness. He was once fined £25 for firing a canon ball from Fort Belan, through the rigging of a passing yacht. He even rigged a shower above one of the estates doors so that when the bell was rung the visitor was showered with cold water.

Close to the fort can be seen Maes Awyr Caernarfon, a private airstrip, once known as RAF Llandwrog. This was a busy fighter and training base used to protect the city of Liverpool during the Second World War. In 1941, the Medical Officer for RAF Llandwrog, a 29 year old Flight Lieutenant called George Graham was to enter into the history books. Alarmed by the number of missing aircraft, injured aircrew and the lack of any properly set up mountain search and rescue scheme, he set up and trained an informal team based on his own pre-war mountaineering experience. It was his enterprise that set up the first RAF Mountain rescue team in Wales. His hard work and dedication was rewarded when he received an M.B.E. in January 1943.

The walk passes the tree shrouded 18th century church of St Baglan (Llanfaglan) with its early Christian and Mediaeval gravestones. Gravestones dating from the 5th and 6th century are being used as a lintel for the north door with the inscription, 'Anatemorus son of Lovernis'.

The walk continues across agricultural land until the halt at Dinas in reached. Here pause to inspect the small but neat museum with the only narrow gauge railway hearse in the world.

The Walk: Exit car park R and along road to button roundabout. Left to edge of quay and to swing bridge. L over bridge then R to follow the coast road. Continue along the road, passing a golf club on left and two small boat yards. **1.** 150 metres after passing white house, 'Cynifryn', L through a kissing gate and up a grassy track to a small church in the trees, (Church of St Baglan). The path now continues crossing the field towards double gates in the wall. Cross over the stile to left of gates. Continue on with hedge on right to kissing gate in the wall. Through this and continue with hedge on right up to a stile situated to L of house. Over this and on with fence on right down to lane. **2.** At lane R for 50 metres then left over a stone stile, a further 10 metres then R passing through a field gate. L crossing the field to pass through a field gate into the next field and cross to a gap in hedges (pass through either the gap, or the kissing gate, which is situated in the left hand corner, in the hedge). Cross the next field to its left hand corner and pass through the kissing gate and over a slate bridge and left along field with hedge on left to a wall corner above small stream. Up the high stone stile and over fence stepping on to old wall and into field. **3.** Up field, with a hedge on R, through gate and over stile close to large house, continue up drive to road. **4.** At road, R for 10 metres, then L over stone stile and into field. Cross field, keeping boundary on L to a metal stile, over this and continue crossing the next field (still with boundary on L) to pass through a wall gap. Continue on along final field to pass through field gate and on to road. R along road passing over river and up towards the edge of the village. 15 metres after passing a road junction sign go L. **5.** Over stile (or through gate) and down the track to pass through kissing gate. Continue on, following the left hand field boundary to another kissing gate. Pass through this and on for 5 metres, now R into field on right. Continue with boundary on R and cross over stile into R/H corner of field. Up field to locate a well-hidden stile, over this and continue on up field to a wooden stile. Over this and follow R/H field boundary to locate another stile. Over this stile. **6.** L to cross field to stile to R of house. Over this and along road to fork (signed 'Lôn Eifion'). L passing the church and at sharp L/H bend continue through fixed barrier and on to Lôn Eifion. Here cross railway line to Dinas.

For those wishing to continue the walk back to Caernarfon, do not cross over line but take the gradually descending Lôn Eifion back into Caernarfon.

Refreshments: Plenty of cafès and pubs exist in Caernarfon itself. The Newborough Arms in Bontnewydd is worth a try.

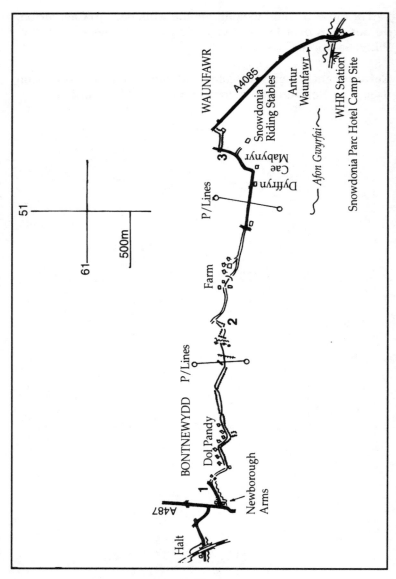

The Gateway to the Mountains
(Bontnewydd Halt to Waunfawr)

Maps: 1:50,000 Landranger sheet 115 Yr Wyddfa *(Snowdon)* and Caernarfon or 1:25,000 Outdoor Leisure sheet 17 Yr Wyddfa *(Snowdon)* and Conwy.
Distance: 3.5 miles/5.6 kilometres.
Height gained: 360ft/110 metres.
Duration: 2.5 hours.
Terrain: Good, passing through meadows also a short stretch of main road walking.
Stations/Halts: Station at Waunfawr, request halt at Bontnewydd.
Car Park: At Snowdonia Parc Hotel (Waunfawr station) GR 526589 and at a small lay-by under bridge at Bontnewydd GR478600.

This short but enjoyable walk is perhaps best done on a summers evening. This will allow the walker to enjoy the hostelry found at the end of the walk. The Snowdonia Parc Hotel boasts its own micro brewery which must be experienced although perhaps this would mean missing the exhibition on show at Antur Waunfawr to the map maker and explorer John Evans and also to the father of modern communications, Gugliemo Marconi.

For this walk you need to dismount at the request halt at Bontnewydd. From here the walk roughly follows the Afon Gwyrfai. The river has its source in Llyn Cwellyn and makes its way down to flow into the sea at Foryd Bay. The railway itself carries on to Waunfawr via Dinas, later following a circular route close to the village of Rhostryfan, where the remains of Tryfan Junction may be seen. The branch line from this location consists almost entirely of one very impressive incline known as the Bryngwyn Branch. The name taken from a small village close by. From the head of the branch line various lines from the Moel Tryfan, Alexandra and Fron quarries fed this link to Dinas and ultimately Caernarfon. This section of the line was opened to goods service on 21st May 1877 and to passenger service on the 1st August of the same year. Unfortunately the 31st December 1913 saw the cessation of passenger traffic to and from Bryngwyn.

As height is gained, Moel Tryfan and the Alexandra quarry complex comes into view, as does the remains of the Bryngwyn incline. To the left of these quarries can be seen the rounded summit of Mynydd Mawr or 'Mynydd Eliffant' as it is called locally (lit. *'elephant mountain'*). Its shape is regarded by many as similar to that of a reclining elephant. The ridge to Mynydd Mawr contains the minor summit of Moel Smytho. On the flanks of Moel Smytho is the village of Rhosgadfan, birthplace and home to the popular Welsh novelist, teacher and literary critic, Kate Roberts.

To the left of the Gwyrfai valley stands Moel Eilio, classed by George Borrow during his journey through Wales as a "noble hill". To its left lies Cefn Du, on the flanks of which are the remains of Marconi's aerial system. The Marconi Company chose this site in 1912, for its Transatlantic Transmitter station. The station and its position were so successful that on 22nd September 1918, the first transmission to Australia was made from here.

The walker now enters the sprawling village of Waunfawr and descends towards the bridge over Afon Gwyrfai. Just before the bridge is reached it is well worth a short diversion to Antur Waunfawr (sign on the R/H side of the road just after the Peugeot body shop). Antur Waunfawr is a successful charitable project overseen by the Welsh Office, aimed at providing employment for mentally handicapped local people. It provides them with an opportunity to give service to the local community in a variety of schemes. In the grounds are a café, a shop selling local produce, a market garden and in the Tŷ Capel, an exhibition is housed. Currently Antur Waunfawr is only open weekdays.

The exhibition to John Evans is located in a converted Calvinistic Methodist Chapel, and what could be more fitting to this Welsh Explorer, as both his father and brothers were prominent ministers here. John Evans was born on 14th April 1770, in the smallholding of Hafod Oleu (located on the Waunfawr to Llanberis road), into a dedicated religious family. At the age of 21, in search of employment he travelled to London. On gaining employment he sought friendship by joining the Madogean society, one he was already familiar with. This was a group of intellectual Welsh set up by the inspiration of Prince Madog. Prince Madog has been credited with the discovery of America in 1170, when he landed his ship the Gwennan Gorn in what is now known as Mobile Bay, Alabama. A visit by General Bowles, a white man declaring himself a native Cherokee chief fuelled Evans' Madog fever and he was soon to leave his homeland, to follow the exploits of his Welsh brethren. It was a strongly held belief that the Welsh Indians known as the Madogwys, were living on the Great Plains close to the Missouri river. During his years of searching for the Madogwys he had many exciting, if not epic, adventures. One of these led to him being imprisoned in St Louis as a British spy. Unfortunately in 1799 at the age of 29, he fell ill and returned to New Orleans where he was diagnosed as having contracted Yellow Fever. He died very shortly after in the Governor's home.

Sadly, his mission to locate the Welsh Indians appears to have been somewhat unsuccessful but his detailed surveys of the Missouri river system were to provide a valuable source of information to President Thomas Jefferson's 1804 expedition. The President asked Meriwether Lewis and William Clark to find a passage from the Great Plains through the Rocky Mountains to the Pacific coast.

In our little expedition it is now time to return to the neat little station close to the Snowdonia Parc Hotel.

25

Walk: Depart from the request halt platform at Bontnewydd, cross the railway line. R following path to road. L along road (river on R) to join main road (A487). R along main road to opposite Newborough Arms, here cross road, taking great care, and down lane between public house and building (sign to pub car park). **1.** 150 metres after pub car park half R down lane and through gate to "Dol Pandy Farm", continue along grassy lane with river on R and pass through next gate (old stone stile by gate). L uphill away from river. Continue along wooded path with wall on R, passing though a number of gates. Path turns L (ruin in front of gate) with wall on R then wall commences to run on L. Over stile and into field, continue with wall on R to field corner. Over metal stile and L passing under power lines and crossing to small stile over fence. Over stile and half L crossing field to another metal stile. Over this and on to cross low wall. **2.** Continue on to wooden gate posts on old wall on L. Through these and half R to metal gate. Through gate and enter lane, R along lane entering farm yard, here R between buildings (yellow footpath signs are in place) crossing outer farmyard and exiting through middle of 3 gates. Continue along walled track passing under power lines and passing Dyffryn and Cae Mabynyr cottages. Along lane passing track to Snowdon Riding stables. **3.** After wooden (paddock type) fence on R, through kissing gate and cross field to white house, keeping low wall on R. Pass in front of house to kissing gate and onto main road (A4085). R down road passing through village of Waunfawr and onto Snowdonia Parc Hotel and station.

Refreshments: Newborough Arms at Bontnewydd and the Snowdonia Parc Hotel and Antur Waunfawr (week days only) in Waunfawr.

For those with energy left it is possible to make this into a circular walk by combining it with the walk Marking the end of

Marking the end of the Mountains

Maps: 1:50,000 Landranger sheet 115 Yr Wyddfa *(Snowdon)* and Caernarfon or 1:25,000 Outdoor Leisure sheet 17 Yr Wyddfa *(Snowdon)* and Conwy.
Distance: 3.5miles/5.6 kilometres.
Height gained: 243ft/74 metres.
Duration: 2 hours.
Terrain: Short section on minor roads, remainder on good tracks.
Station/Halts: Waunfawr station and request halt at Bontnewydd.
Car Park: At the Snowdonia Parc Hotel (Waunfawr) GR 526589 and a parking space for one car can be found close to the railway bridge at Bontnewydd (G.R. 478600)

This picturesque and easy walk leads you away from the high tops of the Gwyrfai valley and heads down towards the coastline of Bae Caernarfon. The walk can be combined with the 'Gateway to the Mountains' to make a gentle walk of some 4 and a half hours. This provides a variety of options allowing the walker to terminate the walk at either the Waunfawr station or at the request halt at Bontnewydd, whilst allowing enough time to enjoy local refreshments before completing the journey back to Caernarfon by train.

As the walk passess around the flanks of Moel Smytho the striking sea cliffs of Yr Eifl come into view. Close to this summit lie the remains of Tre'r Ceiri (lit.*the fort of giants*) one of the finest hill forts in the British Isles. Occupied in A.D.78 the inner walls enclose an area of about 5 acres, within which lie the remains of about 100 huts. The 'Cytiau' *(huts)* are situated in groups on terraces. Specimens of Roman, British, and Celtic pottery, as well as porcelain beads from Egypt, a gold plated bronze fibula of Celtic origin and even specimens of early iron work have been unearthed on this famous site. The nature of the finds and the location of the fort indicate that it was only occupied during the summer season, charcoal remains being very minimal and the site being too damp and bleak for a winter residence.

The imposing quarry of Yr Eifl once exported it's product via the jetty in Trefor. This in itself was not unusual as most quarries in the area relied on sea transport to move the goods to a market However, Yr Eifl quarry transported the stone to the jetty in Trefor by means of an aerial cable way. Eddie Doylerush in his book on aircraft crashes during WW2 tells of an incident involving this cable. On the 9th of September 1943 an Avro Anson from the No3 Air Gunnery School based at Mona on Anglesey, was on a training flight. The pilot was putting the aircraft through its paces near Yr Eifl quarries when he inadvertently clipped the cable with the port wing of the plane. The Anson, now out of control plunged into the sea. Three airmen survived the crash but two tragically died.

As the walk progresses into a hedged lane, a disused railway bridge is crossed. This is the remains of the railway line from Tryfan Junction through to Bryngwyn and on to the Alexandra, Moel Tryfan and Fron quarries. The line serving these quarries consists of one spectacular incline up to the ridge line of Moel Tryfan. The line from this isolated halt was opened for freight to Bryngwyn on the 21st May 1877. It was later opened for passengers on 15th August of the same year. Unfortunately the line was to loose its passenger service over the new year of 1913 and was never to reopen. It retained its freight service for a short period, but even after the reopening of the line in July 1922, the passenger service was never reopened. Just before crossing the next bridge make a short diversion to visit the remains of the Tryfan Junction and to ponder on the remains of the service.

The lane now continues to a junction with the main road at Bontnewydd and on to the request halt for the Welsh Highland Railway.

The Walk: Depart from the car park/railway station at the Snowdonia Parc Hotel at Waunfawr. Go L along the A4085 for

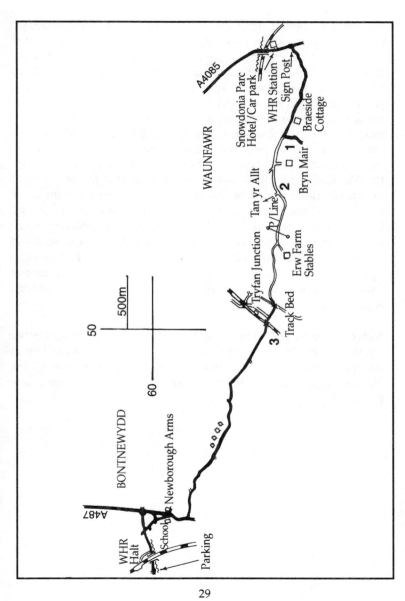

BONTNEWYDD

WHR Halt

A487

School

Newborough Arms

Parking

500m

50

60

Tryfan Junction

Track Bed

3

WAUNFAWR

A4085

Snowdonia Parc Hotel / Car park

WHR Station

Sign Post

Braeside Cottage

1

Bryn Mair

2

Tan yr Allt

P / Line

Erw Farm Stables

100 metres, then R up minor road signposted to Rhosgadfan. Continue up hill until you come to a white cottage on L called "Braeside". Continue for a short distance to a sharp L/H bend. **1.** Here continue on along a lane until it swings L up to Bryn Mair Farm. Here continue on through farm gate. **2.** At junction (with cattle grid on R fork) take L fork and continue on. The track narrows from this location. The track later descends to pass Erw Farm Stables on L. From here the track improves to a lane which passes over the railway bridge for the old Tryfan Junction. A short distance on the lane passes over a bridge for the Welsh Highland Railway. Just before this bridge a short excursion along a lane on the R can be made to the remains of the Tryfan junction station. **3.** Continue along the lane into Bontnewydd where at the A487 go R towards the Newborough Arms. Cross the road to a telephone box. R down steps with old school on L At road junction go L (Golden Cod chip shop opposite) and continue along road until the railway bridge (over road and river) is reached. Here R up path to Bontnewydd request halt.

Refreshments: The Snowdonia Parc Hotel at the start serves bar meals and has its own micro brewery. Antur Waunfawr serves snacks during the week. The end of the walk is near to the Newborough Arms in Bontnewydd and has been a long time favourite.

Cefn Du
(above Waunfawr)

Maps: 1:50,000 Landranger sheet 115 Yr Wyddfa *(Snowdon)* and Caernarfon or 1:25,000 Outdoor Leisure sheet 17 Yr Wyddfa *(Snowdon)* and Conwy.
Distance: 5 miles/8 kilometres.
Height gained: 1033ft/315 metres.
Duration: 2.5 hours.
Terrain: Good, passing through old small holdings and open moor land with bracken.
Stations/Halts: Station at Waunfawr.
Car Park: At Snowdonia Parc Hotel (Waunfawr station) GR 526589.

This excursion allows the walker to dismount from the train at the neat WHR station at Waunfawr, re-opened on the 7th August 2000 after lying derelict for some 59 years. On passing through the station and the Snowdonia Parc Hotel try to avoid the temptation of an early visit to sample the beers from the micro-brewery, savour it until your return.

Pass over the bridge for the WHR and Afon Gwyrfai. Here the river flows on its journey from Llyn Cwellyn to the sea at Foryd, close to Caernarfon. This walk gains height passing through many smallholdings. One of these, Hafod Oleu, was the birthplace of John Evans, the Welsh explorer and mapmaker.

Later you emerge on to the Waunfawr to Llanberis top road, unfortunately no longer a through road and impassable by vehicles. Close to a large plantation a poor path takes the walker towards the quarry tips and then out onto the moorland above the hotpotch of quarry remains. Most of these are the remains of early sites covered over by the more recent excavations. The largest of these remains are the Glynrhonwy Lower and the Glynrhonwy Upper quarries. Glynrhonwy Lower was opened in the early 18th century and was one of the early pioneers for internal railway systems. During the year of 1883, with a work force of only 70, the quarry achieved an output of 1789 tons. The quarry eventually closed in 1930 and the site was taken over by the Ministry of Defence in 1940 as a workshop and storage area for munitions. Many Welsh quarries were converted to this use during the war years. Glynrhonwy Lower was sold off in 1960.

Glynrhonwy Upper was developed in the 19th century and reached its peak with a production of 2181 tons from a 90 strong work force in 1882. The quarry finally closed in 1930.

As the summit of Cefn Du is reached spectacular views of Caernarfon Bar, the Afon Menai and the surrounding mountains come into view. Walking from the summit through a gate in the fence the walker will come to the remains of a brick building. From here, looking down towards Caernarfon, several concrete bases may be seen; these are the remains of a great aerial system. This system, used by the Marconi Company, was used to transmit messages across the Oceans to both the Americas and Australia. On the 22nd September 1918, the first successful transmission to Australia was made from here. The transmission was conducted by the Australian Prime Minister of the day, William Morris Hughes, who was on a brief trip to Britain after visiting the Australian troops in the battlefields of Northern France. On the 4th of December 1921, the Marconi Company invited the *Daily Mail* to send a detailed press transmission direct to their correspondent in Sydney. In 1929, the station was taken over by International Communications Ltd, which was later to become the world-renowned Cable and Wireless Company. With various advances in technology, the site was closed down as a radio station in 1939. The site was visited by Princess Elettra, (Marconi's Daughter) in July 1998. She also took time to visit the home of Sir William Preece at nearby Penrhos, Caeathro. Preece was an outstanding electrical and communications engineer who had acted as mentor to Marconi.

North Wales Narrow Gauge Railways armorial device.

Charles Easton Spooner, 1818-1889. Engineer to the North Wales Narrow Gauge Railways Company and the Ffestiniog Railway.

Abandoned cable drum at the head of the Bryngwyn incline, Welsh Highland Railway.

Welsh Highland Railway.

TRAIN STAFF TICKET.

TRAIN No._____ (UP)

To the ENGINE DRIVER or BRAKESMAN

You are authorised, after seeing the Train Staff colored **Blue** for the Section, to proceed from

Croesor Jct. to Portmadoc (New Station)

and the Train Staff will follow

Signature of person in charge ....

Date .... ,19   (over \

WELSH HIGHLAND RY.
Notice.- This Ticket is issued subject to the conditions on the Time Tables of the Company

370

Portmadoc
TO
BEDDGELERT
First Class
Actual Fare 2/9

WELSH HIGHLAND RY.
Notice.- This Ticket is issued subject to the conditions on the Time Tables of the Company

370

Beddgelert
TO
PORTMADOC
First Class
Actual Fare 2/9

WELSH HIGHLAND RAILWAY
NOTICE—This Ticket is issued subject to the conditions and regulations in the Company's Time Tables Books, Bills and Notices.

329

BEDDGELERT
TO
Portmadoc

THIRD CLASS FARE 1/-

2958
RETURN TICKET
Dinas **3/6** South Snowdon

15   15
16   16
17   17

Bell Punch Company, London

B' 430

Bettws Garmon
Quellyn Lake
South Snowdon
Pitt's Head
Beddgelert
Nantmor
9d.
Hafod Ruffydd
Beddgelert
Nantmor
Hafod y Llyn
Pont Croesor
Portmadoc

30   30
31   31
32   32
33   33
34   34
35   35
36   36
37   37
38   38

WELSH HIGHLAND RAILWAY.

3940
3d.
Waenfawr   Bettws Garmon

1   1
2   2
3   3

WELSH HIGHLAND RAILWAY.

Bell Punch Company, London

Train staff ticket and selection of tickets.

Snowdon Ranger, maker's number 739,
built by the Vulcan Foundry Ltd. in 1875.

Gowrie, maker's number 979,
built by the Hunslet Engine Co. Ltd. in 1908.

Dinas circa 1880. N.W.N.G.R. locomotive *Beddgelert* and train.
Note signal on narrow gauge.

N.W.N.G.R. train at Dinas, about 1895, with *Snowdon Ranger*. The first
coach is a six-wheeled Cleminson design.

Dinas, W.H.R., looking south (August, 1926)

Beddgelert at Dinas, in N.W.N.G. days.

Coaches No. 26, 27, 29 at Dinas, 1942

Dinas, slate being transhipped circa 1920.

Dinas, looking north, from overbridge.

Kerr Stuart diesel locomotive, maker's number 4415, at Dinas in 1928.

Welsh Highland & Ffestiniog Railway wagons and vans with old
N.W.N.G. brake van as used on Bryngwyn Branch.

Dinas in 1925, with *Moel Tryfan* on W.H.R. train

Dinas-Porthmadog train at Waunfawr in 1926.

Russell near Lake Cwellyn, 1936.

Welsh Highland demolition train at Glanrafon siding
near Lake Cwellyn.

Tryfan Junction station, W.H.R., after the line was abandoned.

Final "demolition" passenger train leaving Dinas,
W.H.R., October, 1941.

Lôn Eifion

The station at Dinas today.

Millennium working hard out of Caernarfon.

Mynydd Mawr and Moel Eilio ridge from Bwlch Main.

Mynydd Mawr.

Garn Nantlle from Rhyd-ddu.

Prince

Remains of Hafod above Waunfawr.

Castell Caernarfon

Remains of the tea house on the Rhyd-ddu path.

Enid and the observation car approaching
Yr Wyddfa *(Snowdon)* summit.

Millennium at Caernarfon

Walkers approaching Yr Wyddfa *(Snowdon)* summit from Bwlch Main.

Garn Nantlle from Yr Wyddfa *(Snowdon)* summit.

All that remains is to return to Waunfawr, having completed the walk there is no reason not to sample the local brew from the micro-brewery at the Snowdonia Parc.

The Walk: Depart from the station and cross car park to the main road (A4085). R crossing the bridge and at end of bridge R (footpath sign) up path to kissing gate and road. R along road to pass bungalow 'Cyrnant Lodge' on L. 20 metres after bungalow L up path. At junction on to pass through kissing gate and into a field. Continue on with fence/old wall on R. Pass through another kissing gate. **1.** Pass barn on R, still continuing with wall on R, to pass through wall gap with marker post and on over small stone footbridge. Pass through a further two kissing gates to a lane, here up lane to sharp L/H bend with large rock on bend. Here continue up field with wall on R (if wet descend to R of the rock and then continue up field for a short distance, then pass through wall gap on L and continue up with wall on R) to a stone "lead in" with sign. R into field crossing to a stream. Step over this and pass through kissing gate and along to track. Up track and at fork continue half L passing under power lines to a gate with a stile. Through gate and up to track junction. Here L through gate and cross small stream continuing up track and passing cottages to lane (sign for Tŷ Pella on gate). **2.** R up lane passing underground reservoir on R, at ruin on R (50 metres before edge of plantation) half L up path. From this point continue heading just to L of the quarry tips, trying to keep to the main path and ignoring the many other paths. **3.** Continue climbing past the quarry tips, now on R, to a fenced quarry hole. Here follow fence on L to cross a small section of open moor land to next fence. L following descending fence until it is possible to cross and join an ascending wall/fence. L uphill with wall/fence on R until fence turns L. Follow this to summit. From this point the descent is a reverse of the ascent.

For the more adventurous, from here a diversion can be made down a short path, which descends though a gate and

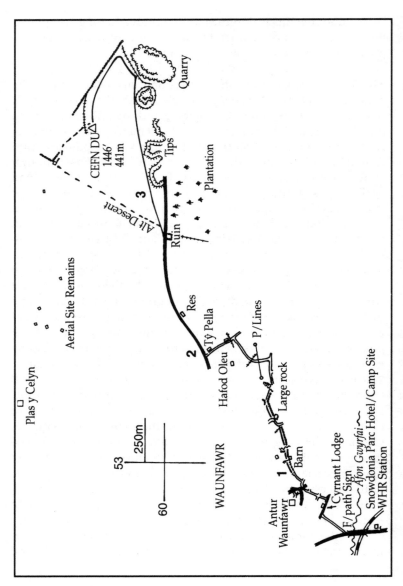

leads to remains of an aerial site. It is possible to regain the road by following one of the many paths down hill, however these can be boggy and deep in heather.

Refreshments: Snowdonia Parc Hotel or Antur Waunfawr (weekdays only).

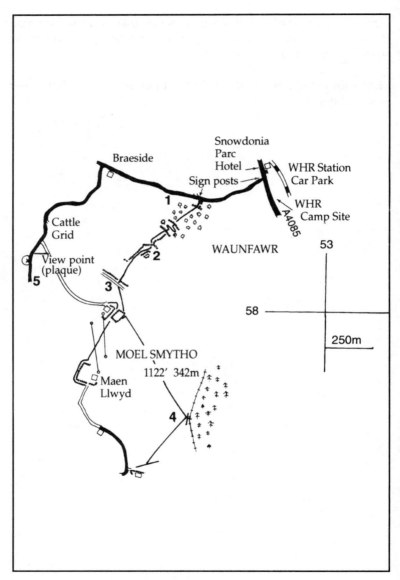

Braeside

Snowdonia
Parc
Hotel

Sign posts

WHR Station
Car Park

WHR
Camp Site

1

A4085

Cattle
Grid

WAUNFAWR

53

View point
(plaque)

2

5

3

58

250m

MOEL SMYTHO

1122′ 342m

Maen
Llwyd

4

Following in the footsteps of Kate Roberts

Maps: 1:50,000 Landranger sheet 115 Yr Wyddfa *(Snowdon)* and Caernarfon or 1:25,000 Outdoor Leisure 17 Yr Wyddfa *(Snowdon)* and Conwy.
Distance: 3.5 miles/5.2kilometres.
Height gained: 712ft/217metres.
Duration: 2.5 hours.
Terrain: Short sections on minor road, wooded hillside and open moorland.
Stations/Halts: Waunfawr station
Car Park: At the Snowdonia Parc Hotel GR 526589.

We are sure that many people enjoying the walk around the flanks of Moel Smytho will delight in the variety of views from this little known top. They may share many of the thoughts that aspiring local Welsh novelist Kate Roberts will have had as she wandered around these hills. Her landscape would have been very different as she gazed at the then thriving Alexandra and Moel Tryfan quarries. Below her, lay the bustling port of Caernarfon, with its busy slate dock full of ships taking slate to the world. In the distance is 'Môn Mam Cymru', Anglesey, the mother of Wales, so called because of the abundance of crops it was able to supply to the rest of Wales.

Kate Roberts was very well known in Welsh literary circles for her novels, short stories and critical judging at the National Eisteddfau. Between 1925 and 1976 she wrote 16 novels and many short stories about the Welsh people and their way of life. She was born into a large family at Bryn Gwyrfai, close to Rhosgadfan, in 1891. Four and a half years later the family moved to near by Caer Gors. 1904 saw her winning a scholarship to the Caernarfon County School. 6 years later she gained a position in the University College of Wales in Bangor, graduating in teaching and music in 1913.

Her first teaching post was at nearby Llanberis, in a primary school. This soon led to promotion and a teaching post in South Wales. In 1925, her first short story, 'O Gors y Bryniau' was published. Following their marriage in 1928, Kate and her husband moved to Dinbych *(Denbigh)* where they were to purchase the local printing works. The works produced the local paper *Y Faner* and the couple ran the paper successfully for many years. Even after the death of her husband in 1946, she continued running the printing works as well as her literary endeavours. In 1950 she was honoured by being made a Doctor of Literature. In 1956 she retired from *Y Faner* but continued with her literary works until her death in 1985.

The walk departs from the Waunfawr Station and ascends up a minor road towards the hamlet of Rhosgadfan. After a short pull up, follow the footpath sign for Y Fron. This takes the walker up a steep hillside shrouded in mixed woodland. This path is one of the many paths created by the quarry workers as they made their way to and from the various places of work. Y Fron quarry is perhaps one of the oldest in this area, as initial operations commenced in about 1830. It was estimated that during its peak in the 1860's, that the output never exceeded 1500 tons with a man power of 100 quarry men. A small quarry in comparison to some of the Llanberis giants.

The path passes through a series of enclosures, which may be the remains of one of the 'Hafoty' or summer residences commonly found in the area. Here shepherds would move their flocks up to the high pastures for the summer.

Later the path crosses the open moorland and ascends the flanks of Moel Smytho to its summit. From here, Kate Roberts, must have sat enjoying the views of Caernarfon, Afon Menai and the Anglesey coastline. The near by Ynys Llanddwyn, with its white washed pilot cottages and light house, was the home of the 5th Century Saint, St Dwynwen, the patron saint of lovers. She fled to the island to escape from an unhappy love affair. On Llanddwyn she built her cell and became an advisor on 'matters of affairs from the heart'.

Later, the path drops from the summit and returns towards Waunfawr. Keep an eye open for a walled area close to a minor road. This area contains the following inscription.

THIS VIEW HAS REFRESHED THE
SPIRIT OF MANY AND INSPIRED THE
WRITINGS OF KATE ROBERTS

This memorial to Kate Roberts is reached by making a short diversion. The road passing the walled area is known as 'Y Lôn Wen' (lit: *the white road*) by the local people of the area.

Continue along Y Lôn Wen before crossing a near by cattle grid and finally descending to the Snowdonia Parc Hotel and Waunfawr station.

The Walk: Depart the car park/railway station at the Snowdonia Parc Hotel and L along the A4085 for 100 metres. R up the road sign posted Rhosgadfan. Continue up the hill until it levels out and on to a stile and signpost indicating 'Y Fron'. **1.** Cross the stile and through the wall gap straight ahead. The path, now faint, runs through bracken. As it enters the trees it climbs steeply up to a wall with a steel ladder. Climb this ladder and continue up the zig zagging path to another stile with another steel ladder. Over this and continue with wall on L (including bend) to a wooden stile. **2.** Over this stile and R to pass through a wall gap and into enclosure. Continue up, passing ruin on L and up to metal gate. Pass through this and onto open moorland. **3.** Go on for 10 metres and cross track, continue on to L/H end of enclosure. Head away from wall corner heading uphill on a meandering track. This path leads to the summit of Moel Smytho. From the summit descend to a forest corner. **4.** At gate and stile into forest, go half R, away from wall and on towards smallholding. At path junction go R down to metalled road. Now R to pass cottages on L. The road now reverts to a track. At Maen Llwyd cottage go L, following a boundary wall until it heads uphill. From here continue following faint track as it passes under power lines and between two enclosures. L along track for a short distance until a viewpoint with a slate plaque can be seen down to the L. At a suitable point descend to the viewpoint. **5.** Exit the viewpoint and go L along the road, later passing over cattle grid and descending to reach the station and carpark.

Refreshments: The Snowdonia Parc Hotel serves bar snacks and has its own micro-brewery. Antur Waunfawr serves snacks but is only open during the week.

Moel Eilio from Waunfawr
to the Snowdon Ranger

Maps: 1:50,000 Landranger sheet 115 Yr Wyddfa *(Snowdon)* and Caernarfon or 1:25,000 Outdoor Leisure sheet 17 Yr Wyddfa *(Snowdon)* and Conwy.
Distance: 7.5 miles/12 kilometres.
Height gained: 1950ft/594 metres.
Duration: 4.5 hours.
Terrain: Good at first passing through a number of small holdings, later on to large open ridge.
Stations/Halts: Station at Waunfawr, halt at Snowdon Ranger.
Car Park: At Snowdonia Parc Hotel (Waunfawr station) and also at Snowdon Ranger Youth Hostel.

The walk departs from the Welsh Highland Railway station at Waunfawr which was re-opened to passenger service on 7th August 2000 after lying derelict for some 59 years. As the walk gains height it passes through a number of smallholdings. These were constructed by the workers employed at the nearby quarries. They were used to either boost their income or just provide fresh produce for their usually large families. One of these smallholdings was Hafod Oleu, the birthplace of John Evans, the Welsh explorer. He was perhaps best known for his attempts to retrace Prince Madog's much earlier exploration of North America.

The footpath joins the old Llanberis to Waunfawr road. This is now only passable by foot or mountain bike, particularly after it passes through the quarry remains of Glynrhonwy Upper, Donnen Las and Bwlch y Groes. Our path now ascends across open moorland and runs alongside the Bryn Mawr land boundary. This is a well preserved bank some 2.5 metres wide and .7 metres high. The bank is not only a parish boundary, it marked a division between the summer grazing lands of the Kings of Gwynedd. As summer was generally the season in which battles were fought, the banks were built to provide protection for the herds of cattle.

Pausing to gain breath, gaze towards the quarrying village of Llanberis and beyond it to Elidir Fawr. Once known as Carnedd Elidir, legend tells us that it was named after Elidir Mwynfawr, son in law to Maelgwn (a prince of Gwynedd). Unfortunately Maelgwn died without a legitimate heir to succeed him and some felt that the right of succession should pass to Elidir Mwynfawr. However, despite him being commander of Maelgwn's forces he was of English descent and many Welshmen felt that it was impossible for an Englishman to receive the title Prince of Wales. This resulted in a fierce battle over the issue during which Elidir was sadly killed. After his death, his followers held him in such esteem, that despite his being English, they constructed a cairn on the summit of Elidir in remembrance. Hence the original name of Carnedd Elidir.

On the flanks of Elidir, can be seen the upper workings of the mighty Dinorwig quarries. These excavations were started as far back as 1770 and the quarries were operational until 1969. Each of the levels were given names and those in the upper reaches of the quarry conjure up thoughts of romantic far away places with names such as Abyssinia, Egypt, Australia and California being given to various workings. Lower down the Assheton Smith family used family christian names for particular workings such as the well known Vivian quarry and the lesser known Harriet, Alice and Moses quarries. The quarry men had their own names for some levels with names such as Llangristiolus and Bonc Refail to remind them of their homes and families. In its heyday the quarry employed some 3,000 men and achieved an output of 100,000 tons.

The dexterity of the workforce was so great that during the height of the slate boom a hospital was built and staffed to deal with the medical needs of the employees and their families. In one particular accident a quarryman lost both his arms, a terrible injury and one which would have made life very difficult in those days. However artificial limbs were designed by the quarry doctor and manufactured by the blacksmith. Once fitted, these devices enabled the poor man to eat unaided, and of more importance, remove his hat when entering chapel.

As the walk follows the broad ridge, views of Llyn Cwellyn can be seen. One of the possible translations for this name is thought to be lake of the baskets or creels. These may have been used to trap fish at the lakes' outfall, especially as Llyn Cwellyn was one of the few lakes to contain Arctic Char. Llyn Padarn, near Llanberis and Llyn Bodlys in the Rhinog range are the only other lakes to have contained Arctic Char. The lake is over 120ft deep and was converted into a resevoir for the Caernarfon district in 1976.

The crags, which dominate the far shore of the lake, are known as Castell Cidwm. Its vertical flanks are a Mecca for hard rock climbers, especially the pioneers of the 60's. There is a photograph taken by Edgar Siddal of the legendary Joe Brown. He is depicted climbing the route 'Tramgo' on Castell Cidwm and the photograph is featured on the signs outside Joe Browns' shops. Sadly, the crags have lost favour with the modern climber and it is unlikely you will see anyone on these steep walls.

The path now descends from the summit of Foel Goch down to Bwlch Maesgwm. The Bwlch was the high point in a drover's route and burial road, which connected Rhyd-ddu and Llanberis. Continue down to the Snowdon Ranger path and eventually to the youth hostel.

The Walk: Depart from the station and cross car park to the main road (A4085). R crossing the bridge and at end of bridge R (footpath sign) up path to kissing gate and road. R along road to pass bungalow 'Cyrnant Lodge' on L. 20 metres after bungalow L up path. At junction on to pass through kissing gate and into a field. Continue on with fence/old wall on R. Pass through another kissing gate. **1.** Pass barn on R, still continuing with wall on R, to

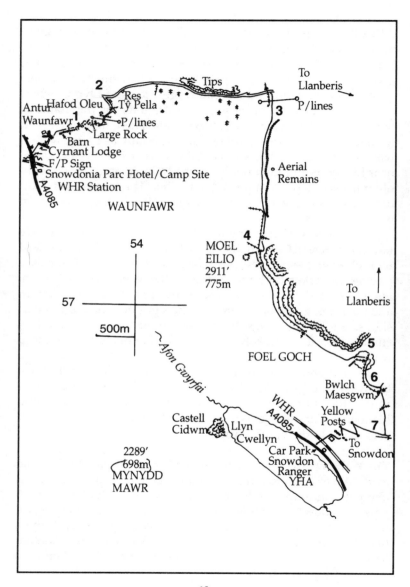

pass through wall gap with marker post and on over small stone footbridge. Pass through a further two kissing gates to a lane, here up lane to sharp L/H bend with large rock on bend. Here continue up field with wall on R (if wet descend to R of the rock and then continue up field for a short distance, then pass through wall gap on L and continue up with wall on R) to a stone "lead in" with sign. R into field crossing to a stream. Step over this and pass through kissing gate and along to track. Up track and at fork continue half L passing under power lines to a gate with a stile. Through gate and up to track junction. Here L through gate and cross small stream continuing up track and passing cottages to lane (sign for Tŷ Pella on gate). **2.** Up lane passing underground reservoir on R. Pass between slate tips and plantation, lane now becoming a track. Continue along track to fork, here take R fork and head to gate with stile on skyline. **3.** Over stile and continue on for 20 metres. Up rough track (closest to fence on R) passing under power lines. Continue following rough track, low wall on L, later a fence comes in from R. Continue uphill with this fence later crossing over stile. Continue to next stile and over this to summit. **4.** Return to stile (do not cross) and turn R, now with fence on L. Over next stile and follow fence along broad ridge crossing another stile at fence termination. **5.** Continue along ridge, as the ascent to Foel Goch is made a wall/fence will come in from R. Continue along with fence on R to a set of stiles. Cross stile directly in front, then R following fence (still on R) descending to Bwlch, gate and set of stiles. **6.** Pass through gate and down path, over another stile (later passing a convenient seat for a view point) down to Snowdon Ranger path (sign for Llanberis). **7.** R along path later descending a number of zig zags marked with yellow poles. Pass through gate and continue down to farm, then L down track to road.

Refreshments: Castell Cidwm or Antur Waunfawr (week days only).

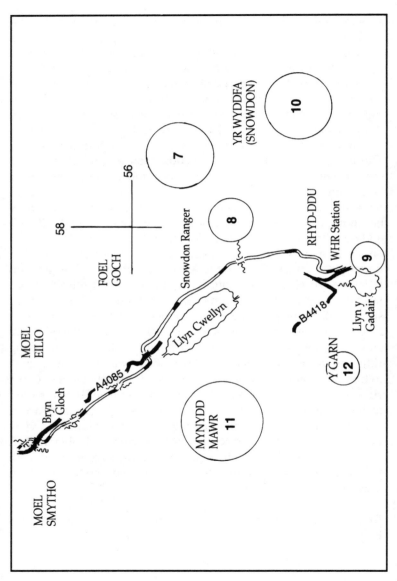

Yr Wyddfa *(Snowdon)* from the Snowdon Ranger

Maps: 1:50,000 Landranger sheet 115 Yr Wyddfa *(Snowdon)* and Caernarfon or 1:25,000 Outdoor Leisure sheet 17 Yr Wyddfa *(Snowdon)* and Conwy.

Distance: 8 miles/6.4 kilometres.

Height gained: 3085ft/940 metres.

Duration: 6 hours.

Terrain: Good hard surface on open moor land then ascending broad rocky ridges.

Stations/Halts: The Snowdon Ranger station.

Car Park: Close to Snowdon Ranger Youth Hostel G.R.563551.

The Snowdon Ranger path to Yr Wyddfa's summit has a diverse and interesting history. It departs from the banks of Llyn Cwellyn close to the aptly named Youth Hostel. The path was a popular guided route well into the 20th century, particularly as it was considered very foolish for anyone to climb a mountain without a guide. The original guides to the area were local men, usually shepherds, employed by the travellers to guide them safely across the barren unexplored mountains. The origin of the name Snowdon Ranger is open to debate with some believing it refers to a local guide whilst others think it refers to the building.

The first account of a guided ascent of Yr Wyddfa was given by Thomas Johnson. In 1639, he came to the area in search of plant specimens and employed a local boy to guide him on what appears to have been the Beddgelert Path out of Rhyd-ddu. No further documentary evidence of ascents can be found until 150 years later, when mention is made of guides being employed by the hotels in Caernarfon. Later, the hotels in Beddgelert began to employ guides and in general the route taken up Snowdon was the path we now know as the Snowdon Ranger.

The Youth Hostel was mentioned in 1770 by Joseph

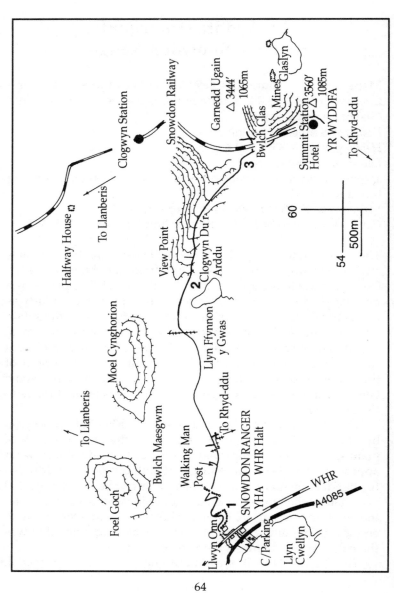

Caradock in his 'Letters from Snowdonia'. In the letters he described the building as a small thatched hut inhabited by a labouring man with six or seven children. He stayed overnight and was entertained by a blind harpist. In 1798 there was an account by Miss Bowdler and Elizabeth Smith who both set out at 1 o'clock in the morning with the Snowdon Ranger to experience the sunrise over the Welsh landscape. Was this Snowdon Ranger the guide Robert Evans? The building at the time was known as the Saracens Head.

In 1805, an account by Richard Yates states that he was not very pleased with his accommodation at the Snowdon Ranger. He describes it as an alehouse on the banks of Llyn Cwellyn whose rooms were so foul that he and his companion found their bedding flea and bug ridden. They were forced to rise early for their ascent. The landlord at this time was a Mr Masters.

In 1854, when George Borrow was on his journey through Wales, he described the Snowdon Ranger as a farmhouse that supplied occasional accommodation. The landlord of the time was a John Morton, who insisted to Borrow that he was the original Snowdon Ranger and that the property was named after him. After this period the accommodation appears to improve, as Murray in 1874, describes the Snowdon Ranger as a solitary but comfortable little Inn much patronised by anglers. The Landlord not only acted as a guide to Snowdon's summit but also an adviser and boat hirer to the fishing fraternity on Llyn Cwellyn. Abel and Heywood's 1890 guidebook advertises the hotel as centrally situated for tourists and cyclists on the main road from Beddgelert to Caernarfon. For a short time after this period the building was used as a chapel and then reverted back to being an inn. Much later it was purchased by the Youth Hostel Association, in which role it continues to the present day.

In the late 1770's to the early 1800's miners and shepherds would supplement their meagre wages by carrying dressed copper ore from the mines in the Glaslyn Bowl (on the northern flanks of Yr Wyddfa) up 1000ft to Bwlch Glas and then with the assistance of horses, skid the load down to the Saracens Head (Snowdon Ranger) to where it could be transported to the quays of Caernarfon for export.

As the path gradually ascends away from the Youth Hostel it passes close to a farm outbuilding. On the end of this building, the remains of a water wheel can be seen. Wheels of this type were used for the production of cattle food when only poor quality hay was available. Gorse and furze were gathered as a valuable spring food and they were fed into the bruising mills driven by the water mill. This reduced the prickly points of the plants sufficiently for it to be used as foodstuff. This foodstuff was used in the proportion of 1 furze, 2 hay and 1 potato for the cattle food.

Soon the walker can pause to enjoy the views from the summit of Clogwyn Du'r Arddu. A Mecca for rock climbers, this fearsome crag was made popular by the exploits of Joe Brown and Don Whillans. However the earliest people to ascend this crag were a group of clerics in search of valuable plant specimens. One of the most well known of these clerics was the Rev W Bingley, who was to become one of the pioneers of rock climbing. Just after the crags of Clogwyn Du'r Arddu, the Snowdon Mountain Railway is joined and the path runs along side the track before bearing off to the summit of Snowdon itself. Both the railway and the summit have fascinating stories of their own well documented in other publications.

To return, the path retraces it steps back to the Youth Hostel.

The Walk: Exit car park and cross road to ascending path indicated with footpath and bridle way signs (Cae'r Orsaf) to station. L along the path to a farm lane, now R ascending lane to farm buildings. **1.** 10 metres after buildings R (words 'Path' on rock), the path now zig zags up hillside later to pass walking man sign post indicating Llanberis. Eventually the path crosses a fence with a gate and stile, close to the lake of Llyn Ffynnon y

Gwas. From this point the path becomes steep up the flanks of Clogwyn Du'r Arddu. Along here a viewpoint enables the walker to enjoy views into Cwm Brwynog and down to Llanberis. **2.** From the viewpoint the path ascends diagonally across the flanks of Garnedd Ugain to join the Snowdon Railway track. Here a slate obelisk at Bwlch Glas indicates the path. **3.** Cross the line with care and continue up the grassy bank to join the Llanberis path, soon to meet the path from the Horseshoe and the Miners paths again indicated by an obelisk. From here continue up to the summit.

The descent route retraces the ascent route so descend to the obelisk indicating the junction with the Horseshoe and Miners path at Bwlch Glas then descend half L to the railway track. Cross this at the obelisk indicating the Snowdon Ranger path and return via the ascent route.

Refreshments: Pub grub can be obtained at the Cwellyn Arms in Rhyd-ddu and food is also available at the Castell Cidwm Hotel, situated on the banks of Llyn Cwellyn. In the village of Beddgelert there are numerous public houses and cafes, the Antique shop being open all year round for snacks and drinks. Of course, there is the 'hotel' on Yr Wyddfa's summit, which is open for refreshments during the summer season.

Rhyd-ddu and Llyn y Gadair

Maps: 1:50,000 Landranger sheet 115 Yr Wyddfa *(Snowdon)* and Caernarfon or 1:25,000 Outdoor Leisure sheet 17 Yr Wyddfa *(Snowdon)* and Conwy.
Distance: 5 miles/8 kilometres.
Height gained: 360ft/109 metres.
Duration: 3 hours.
Terrain: Some marshy areas which can be wet, also where streams cross the foot path on the flanks of Y Garn.
Stations/Halts: Rhyd-ddu station.
Car Park: Located to the south end of Rhyd-ddu (closest to Beddgelert) on A4085 is a pay and display car park G.R.571525.

The North Wales Narrow Gauge Company terminated its extension to the 'Moel Tryfan' undertaking at Rhyd-ddu. The reason for this extension was to ease the transport problems for Glanrafon Quarry and other quarries. With the construction of the station, which became known as the 'Snowdon Station', a passenger service was started in May 1881. Unfortunately the station had a short life span, on 31st October 1916, during the hostilities of the First World War, the passenger service to the station was withdrawn. Service to the station was re-opened on 31st July 1922, with the extension of the track to Beddgelert opening on the 1st June 1923. Unfortunately at this point in time the Quarries were in decline and were no longer a viable proposition. The loss of trade from the Quarries on the railway line led to the closure of the station to passengers (of what had become a summer only service). Passenger traffic ceased on 26th September 1936 and freight ceased to be carried on 19th June 1937. By this time all the quarries in the area had closed.

The path crosses a marshy area where the remains of a branch line constructed from the station to the Llyn y Gadair Quarry can be seen. This project on the banks of Llyn y Gadair was never completed, the quarry opening in 1885 and closing in 1920.

High above the forest, stands Moel Hebog and situated on its northern flanks is the summit of Moel yr Ogof (bare flat topped mountain of the cave). Here is what is thought to be the hiding place of the Welsh Prince Owain Glyndŵr, who was reputed to have sought refuge here in 1410 after he refused to yield to the English forces after his long and hugely effective independece campaign. Living the life of a hunted outlaw, he was never caught, not once betrayed and moved from being a man to become a myth. He never died in the Welsh folk memory and still sleeps in one of his many caves in the highlands of Wales, still waiting for his finest hour. Later the path takes the walker on to the main road to walk for a short while in the direction of Rhyd-ddu. At the gate of Ffridd Uchaf farm, on the opposite side of the road can be seen a rock known as 'Pitts Head'. This is a large rock, which was noticed by early travellers in the area. They were struck by the profile, which was said to be similar to that of William Pitt. William Pitt became Prime Minister in 1783 at the age of 24 and was to hold office for 17 years.

The highest point of the walk above Ffridd Uchaf farm is where it joins the footpath to Yr Wyddfa's summit. That is for another day for our path returns to Rhyd-ddu passing the long disused Ffridd Quarry.

The outdoor centre in Rhyd-ddu village was once the Schoolhouse and the home of one of the most outstanding literary figures in Wales. It was home to poet, essayist and literary critic Syr T. H. Parry-Williams (1887-1975). He came to prominence through the then unprecedented feat of winning both Crown and Chair in the National Eisteddfod at Wrecsam in 1912 and again in Bangor in 1915.

The farm of Clogwyn y Gwin, close to Rhyd-ddu has a macabre connection with the final shot to be fired in the battle of Waterloo. The tale tells that after the battle itself was over, the son of the farmer of Clogwyn y Gwin was lying wounded, waiting for medical help. Amongst the dead and dying, with a bullet in his kneecap, he saw an old woman moving amongst

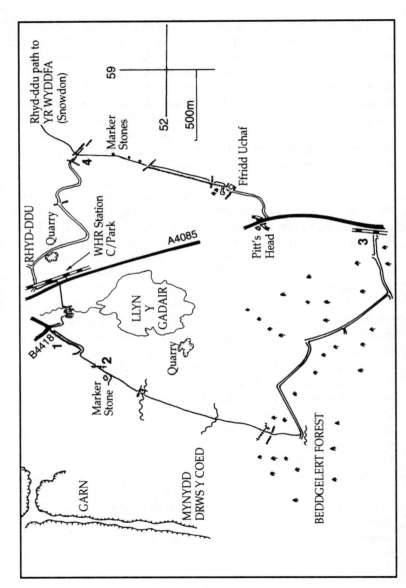

the corpses removing them of whatever valuables they possessed, dispatching those who still had breath with a mallet. She saw the son raise himself and nodded as if to say 'I'll deal with you later'. Struggling, he lifted himself up enough to raise his musket, and taking careful aim, shot her dead. That was reputed to be the very last shot fired during the battle of Waterloo.

The Walk: From the car park, take the exit closest to the village of Rhyd-ddu, and cross the main road (A4085) to pass through a kissing gate (indicated by a walking man sign). Cross the marshy ground, on slate slabs, heading towards a white cottage in the dip. Go L to follow the river with handrail on R, and R over bridge. Over stile and cross over track following white arrows to rejoin track further on. Half R along track and up towards road. **1.** Through the gate and L through another gate (bridleway sign) along path with wall on R. Path bends L away from wall and ascends up to gate with stile. **2.** Cross over stile and continue on along gently ascending path, passing rock with painted arrows (do not take any paths ascending up to Y Garn). Path leads towards forest. Pass through a gate and continue on along gently ascending path. Path crosses hillside and later fords a stream. Pass through a gate (with stile) to enter forest. Pass through wall gap and continue on to track (boulders on opposite side of track). L down track and eventually down to main road. **3.** L along main road to Ffridd Uchaf (bus stop and Snowdon signs). R up track to farm. Enter yard and half R passing between buildings to top R/H corner. Through gate and up field with wall on L. Continue through kissing gate and then over stile. Continue up field, path faint at first, then following a line of marker stones to bear half L to meet track. **4.** L down track passing remains of quarry on L, and onto track junction with swing gate. Half L down to field gate. Through field gate and L to car park

Refreshments: The Cwellyn Arms in Rhyd-ddu is closest and has interesting beers and an unusual atmosphere.

The Rhyd-ddu Burial Road
to the Snowdon Ranger

Maps: 1:50,000 Landranger sheet 115 Yr Wyddfa *(Snowdon)* and Caernarfon or 1:25,000 Sheet 17 Yr Wyddfa *(Snowdon)* and Conwy.
Distance: 3.5 miles/6 kilometres.
Height gained: 620ft/190 metres.
Duration: 2.5 hours.
Terrain: Open moorland which can be wet in places.
Station/Halts: Rhyd-ddu and Snowdon Ranger.
Car Park: Rhyd-ddu car park (Pay and Display) G.R.571525, and just opposite Snowdon Ranger Youth Hostel G.R.563551.

This path, which runs from Rhyd-ddu to Llanberis is thought to be one of the old 'burial roads'. This was due to the fact that there was no consecrated ground in the village of Rhyd-ddu. In order to obtain a Christian burial the deceased had to be transported over the open moorland to the pass at Bwlch Maesgwm and then down into Llanberis for internment. The path, a little indistinct at first negotiates some marshy ground towards the remains of the Rhos Clogwyn quarry. On the right of the path a small tower can be seen on a hillock and this is the remains of the gunpowder store for the Ffridd Quarries. Within a short distance of gaining the Welsh Highland Railway track the path angles away at the base of an incline from the Rhos Clogwyn quarry. This quarry, developed in the late 1880's transported its slate to Caernarfon by horse and cart; unfortunately work in the quarry was to cease just shortly after it was connected to the North Wales Narrow Gauge Railway in May 1881. The quarry saw a short lived revival between 1920 and 1930.

The path now marked by a series of 'walking man posts' gently ascends between rocky outcrops passing the remains of a 'Hendref' or winter dwelling. Here, shepherds would bring

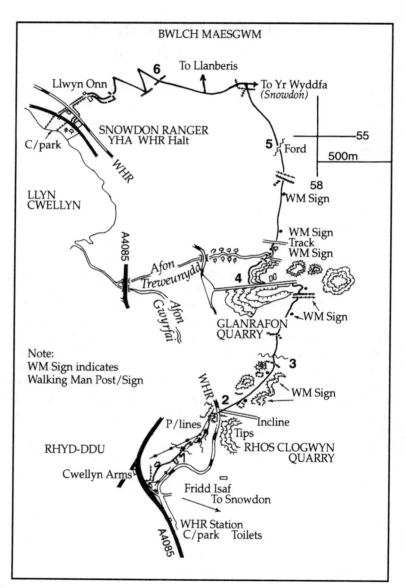

their families and flocks from the summer grazing areas higher up the mountains to winter in the relative shelter of the valley.

The path now crosses into the Glanrafon quarry whose open cast workings can be explored provided great care is taken. This was the largest quarry in the area, being developed from a small scale in the 1870's, to a flourishing quarry by 1882. With a production of over 1,700 tons of slate and a workforce of 250 men, the quarry profited due to its connection to the North Wales Narrow Gauge Railway in 1881. The quarry closed in 1915 never to re-open, its fate sealed by the bursting of the dam wall of Llyn Treweunydd in that same year. The water from the reservoir supplied the power to operate much of the equipment in the quarry and was an essential part of the workings, its demise left the quarry without a power source.

The near by Llyn Glas is associated with a sad story regarding the loss of one of the mountain guides. The guide known as 'Guto Satan', was returning from a wild night on Snowdon's summit in March of 1891. He had been stocking the summit accommodation with provisions but had failed to return home. A search was organised but was unsuccessful in locating him and it was not until June of that year, after renewed requests through the local paper, that the search was re-instated. Sadly his body was located at the base of one of the gullies close to the lake.

The path now crosses open moorland to join the Snowdon Ranger path on its way down from the summit. Descend the flanks of Foel Goch to return to the Snowdon Ranger and Llyn Cwellyn.

The Walk: Depart from the station and car park and follow the line towards the Rhyd-ddu path to Yr Wyddfa's summit (passing toilets on L). Opposite gate on R signposted for the summit, take lane on L passing down between houses. Just before main road R up to and through kissing gate. The path from this point is not very clear but a good indication of its direction is by following the power lines towards the large quarry. **1.** The faint path passes the fenced in remains of a small disused quarry, from here continue to cross open ground following power lines crossing over wooden and stone bridges. The path passes around the back of a small rocky outcrop and ascends up to a gate onto the railway line. **2.** Cross the line and through a wooden gate at the base of the incline, here half L heading towards the gap between two rocky outcrops, passing ruin on R. Continue up hill to pass walking man sign and broken wall on L. FROM THIS LOCATION THE PATH IS VERY WELL MARKED BY "WALKING MAN" SIGNS. **3.** Pass through wall gap and cross boggy area ascending to pass walking man sign and ruin on L, heading in the direction of the obvious notch in the quarry skyline. Cross over stile over fence and stile over wall. The path now ascends a waste tip passing further walking man signs and then descending a grassy incline passing old splitting sheds. **4.** Through wall gap and R to follow the base of the waste tips, continue following the base of the tips as the path now starts to ascend to a small stile over a fence. The path drops to steel bridge over a stream, cross this and up to a walking man sign by a tree. Cross the track and head up to a walking man sign on hillock (150 metres). Continue ascending towards L/H edge of wall on skyline. On gaining the wall pass through wall gap and over stile, faint path continues uphill. **5.** Cross stream at ford and continue on to cross stile at wall and fence junction. Cross to the Snowdon Ranger path. **6.** Go L and the path now descends down a series of zigzags to farm buildings. L to pass building with old water wheel and down towards the main road. At bottom of field go L and on towards the Snowdon Ranger halt and car park.

Refreshments: Castell Cidwm Hotel at the north end of Llyn Cwellyn has superb views to go with your coffee. In Rhyd-ddu village is the Cwellyn Arms, whilst the village of Beddgelert has public houses and shops open all year round. The Antique Shop with its Tea Room is an old favourite.

Yr Wyddfa *(Snowdon)* Summit via the Rhyd-ddu path

(Beddgelert path)

Maps: 1:50,000 Landranger sheet 115 Yr Wyddfa *(Snowdon)* and Caernarfon or 1:25,000 Outdoor Leisure sheet 17 Yr Wyddfa *(Snowdon)* and Conwy.
Distance: 7.5 miles / 12 kilometres.
Height gained: 2935ft / 894 metres.
Duration: 5 hours at least.
Terrain: Good going from a broad ridge to a narrow ridge with some easy scrambling on narrow ridge.
Car Park: At the station in Rhyd-ddu in a pay and display car park G.R.571525.

The path from Rhyd-ddu to Yr Wyddfa's summit is confusingly called the Beddgelert path. The path departs from Rhyd-ddu station, the original terminus of the North Wales Narrow Gauge Railway, and was initially known as the Snowdon station but was later re-titled the Snowdon South station. This terminus was opened on 14th May 1881 and boasted a coach service connecting it to the village of Beddgelert. On the 31st October 1916 the station was closed to passengers only to be re-opened again on 31st July 1922. In the following year, on the 1st of June 1923 a connecting service to Porthmadog commenced. Unfortunately the services were unreliable and intermittent, with the railway being closed to passenger service in 1936 and closed to freight in 1937.

Passing through the gate to Ffridd Isaf, you pass close to a round tower style building. This was used as the magazine for the storage of explosives for the nearby Ffridd quarry. Later the path turns off the Cwmllan quarry access road and climbs the flanks of the Llechog ridge. Just before the first rocky step, the remains of a 'Tea shop' can be seen. This was constructed during

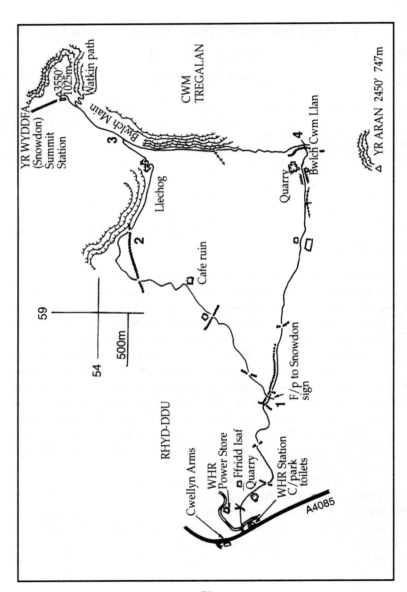

the days of guided ascents to Snowdon's summit, and allowed walkers to enjoy the delights of afternoon tea with spectacular views over Afon Gwyrfai and the valley.

The ascent of the Llechog ridge provides views of Cwm Clogwyn and its many lakes. Moel Cynghorion and Moel Eilio can be seen, whilst during the summer months the locomotives of the Snowdon Mountain railway will be seen winding their tortuous route to the summit. Later as the view opens to the south the splendid valley of Cwm Tregalan will be seen. On the valley floor lies the remains of the unproductive South Snowdon slate quarry. Also dotted about the hillsides of Yr Aran and Lliwedd are the remains of Hafod y Llan copper and lead mines. The mines were at their peak in 1847 when the area saw 150 tons of copper and 30 tons of lead extracted. The major problem for both the slate and copper/lead mines was the difficulty and cost of transportation to the nearest ports.

Cwm Tregalan is also famous in Arthurian legends. Arthur was camped at Dinas Emrys, when he received word that his nephew Mordred, with his Saxon army, was camped at Cwm Tregalan. Not wishing to be ambushed in the narrow confines of Cwm Llan, Arthur marched his troops around Yr Aran and through the pass at Bwlch Cwm Llan. This surprise attack forced Mordred and his army up and over Bwlch y Saethau. A fierce battle followed, hence the literal translation of this place as *Pass of the Arrows*. It was here that Arthur met his untimely death. Legend states that his body was laid to rest under a large cairn, Carnedd Arthur. Waiting for Arthur's return, his knights sleep in a cave on Lliwedd's steep northern face. From here Bedwyr, Arthur's trusted knight cast the mighty sword Excaliber into the deep waters of Llyn Llydaw.

What we do know for certain is that in 1860, some miners climbed a route known as 'slanting gully' to try and locate Arthur's gold. This is graded severe in modern climbing and for many years their claims were ridiculed because of the difficulty of the route. That was until 1900, when a successful attempt of 'slanting gully' discovered a stemple high up the route. A stemple was a spike used by miners to force holes in the slate prior to placing explosives. This tool was found firmly hammered into the rock on the crux of the climb.

On the summit of Yr Wyddfa is the hotel, at which you may be able to play spot the mountaineer or purchase some refreshments (only in the summer months). There has been a building at this location since 1820 when a small hut was constructed from stone. This hut was maintained by the professional guides who catered for the many visitors climbing the mountain from Llanberis. 1890 saw the opening of a wooden hut called the 'Owens and Roberts Bazaar', which provided refreshments and beds for the Victorian adventurers. The first hotel to be owned by the Snowdon Mountain Railway company was built in 1897. The present building was constructed in 1934 and was designed by Sir Clough Williams Ellis (of Portmeirion fame). It also offered beds and refreshments until its closure in 1942 when it was occupied by the Air Ministry. Subsequently, the Admiralty and finally the War Department held residence during its use as part of an Atlantic Radar chain for Coastal Command. Two massive generators were installed and crews assigned, but the project was eventually cancelled. Snowdonia National Park Authority purchased the building in 1983 with the Railway Company providing refreshments. The building was refurbished in 1988 and is open from early spring to early October. In 2000, the summit of Yr Wyddfa and large estates were bought by the National Trust with public donations and there are ambitious plans for careful developments at the summit.

The return is made by descending the complete ridge of Bwlch Main to Bwlch Cwm Llan. Then through the Bwlch Cwm Llan quarries and via the quarry access road to return to Rhyd-ddu.

The Walk: Exit the car park along track passing toilet on L, continue on until a gate on R is reached (sign Ffridd Isaf). R passing through gate and along track. At fork half R through swing gate and continue up track with quarry hole on R. **1.** After crossing over a number of stiles the track levels out. L though a kissing gate, with sign 'Footpath to Snowdon'. Continue up paved footpath passing through gap in low wall. Continue ascending to cross stile in high wall. The path is later marked by cairns, then through kissing gate at which point the path makes a large loop and passes through another kissing gate in the same wall but higher up the ridge. **2.** Continue along broad ridge to a large fence post, here the path climbs steadily following a zigzag fence line. At the termination of the fence the path crosses a steep slope before joining the narrow ridgeline. **3.** At the point where the path crosses from the left hand side of the ridge to the right hand side, make a mental note of your location. You will need to return to this point. The path now crosses the ridge ascending up the right hand flank, later passing the obelisk indicating the Watkin path. Continue up to the summit of Yr Wyddfa. From the summit descend back to where you crossed over the ridge. At this point follow the ridgeline itself. The path descends over a number of rocky steps and later over a stile crossing a fence. Continue descending to an old wall. Here at its lowest point go R across wall. **4.** The path runs through quarry remains soon to meet a fence on L. Continue following this until just past a stile, then half R down path, which soon becomes a broad track. This leads you back to Rhyd-ddu.

Refreshments: Pub Grub is available from the Cwellyn Arms in Rhyd-ddu, also refreshments at Castell Cidwm hotel situated on the banks of Llyn Cwellyn. In the village of Beddgelert there are a number of Public Houses and Cafes. The Antique Shop/Café near the bridge is open all year round for snacks and drinks.

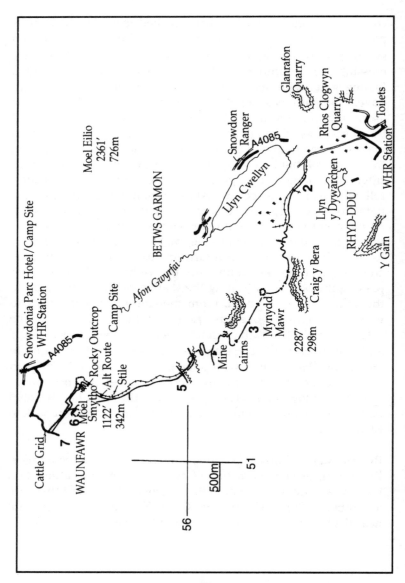

Mynydd Mawr ('Mynydd Eliffant')

Maps: 1:50,000 Landranger sheet 115 Yr Wyddfa *(Snowdon)* and Caernarfon or 1:25,000 Outdoor Leisure sheet 17 Yr Wyddfa *(Snowdon)* and Conwy.

Distance: 7miles/11.25 kilometres.

Height gained: 1663ft/507 metres.

Duration: 4.5 hours.

Terrain: Good grassy ridges (steep in places) with some scree and a pleasant moorland section at the end of the walk.

Stations/Halts: Waunfawr Station and also at Rhyd-ddu.

Car Park: At the Snowdonia Parc in Waunfawr GR 526589 and at Rhyd-ddu near the A5045 in a pay and display G.R. 571525.

This walk passes through the tiny village of Rhyd-ddu with its distinctive Cwellyn Arms Inn, then up on to the flanks of Mynydd Mawr. The mountain is often referred to as Mynydd Eliffant due to its resemblance to a sleeping elephant, but this can only be seen when viewing it from the Caernarfon area.

The footpath ascends through the forest on to the ridge of Bwlch Moch, from where there are splendid views of Y Garn and the Nantlle ridge. Below and to the left can be seen the lake, Llyn y Dywarchen (lit: *the lake with the floating island*) whose mysteries have fascinated travellers for many years. During his travels in Wales in 1188, Giraldus Cambrensis noted in his journal the strange phenomenon of a floating island, only to be held in position at the mercy of the wind. In 1698, the famous astronomer Edmond Halley visited the lake to witness this mysterious island for himself. He even pushed the island out into the middle of the lake; swimming out after it to make sure it really did float. Pennant investigated it in 1786 noting that cattle suddenly found themselves afloat in the middle of the lake. A painting by the 18th century artist Richard Wilson shows a man with a pole on the island, indicating its mobility. Records indicate the island was still in place in 1931.

One account of the creation of the island is the local folklore regarding the Tylwyth Teg *(the fairy folk)*. A local shepherd from near by Drws y Coed farm used to hide in the reeds close to the lake to watch the Tylwyth Teg. He fell in love with a most beautiful young girl. One evening he chose to abduct her and he took her to his farm cottage, where he kept her locked up until he could win over her affections. His patience finally paid off, but when he asked for her hand in marriage she refused, offering only to be his servant until he could find out her name. One evening he happened to overhear a group of Tylwyth Teg who were returning from a local market. They were discussing the missing girl and the farmer heard her name mentioned. Slowly gaining her confidence, she agreed to marry him on the condition that he never struck her with iron. Unfortunately, one day whilst out riding, her horse stumbled and sank into a bog. Her husband struggled to release the stricken beast and in the confusion accidentally caught his wife on the leg with the iron bridle. The law of the Tywyth Teg is such that after being struck by iron a wife can no longer remain married to an earthly being. So, to enable her to remain close to her husband, they created a floating island in the lake, where she could sit and converse with her loved one, whilst he sat on the shore. It was by this means that the couple lived happily until finally the shepherd of Drws y Coed passed away and into local folk lore. This account of the island's creation is far more entertaining than the probable explanation, which relies on methane gas keeping the island afloat.

The breached dam, which can be seen close to the lake, also held a second lake known as Bwlch y Moch. The dam was constructed in 1840 to provide power for the nearby Drws y Coed copper mine. Close to these two lakes are the remains of the cottage, Llwyn y Forwyn. This was an early home of an incredibly talented woman called Marged uch Ifan. An athlete, fisherwoman, hunter, wrestler and musician of note, she moved from the Nantlle area, where she had been running a public house. She was to provide a similar service for the nearby copper mines. Later, in the 1700's, she moved to Llanberis where she secured a contract to transport copper ore from the mines at Nant Peris, crossing Llyn Peris and Llyn Padarn and on to a small dock at Afon Rhyddallt at the head of Llyn Padarn. The ore was transported from here down to Caernarfon.

Below the crumbling precipitous cliffs of Craig y Bere the remains of the Drws y Coed copper mines can be seen. Nantlle vale produced most of the copper ore raised in Snowdonia and Drws y Coed was probably one of the oldest of these mines. Records indicate that the mine was visited in 1284 by Edward the 1st. By the time it closed in 1930, it was one of the most profitable in Britain, with in excess of 30,000 tons of ore being extracted from the workings, of which some were sunk to a depth of 600ft.

The path from the summit descends towards Afon Menai and has views across to Anglesey, later the path passes close to a trial copper mine close to the edge of the Cwm Du crags.

The Walk: Exit car park/station at Rhyd-ddu and walk along, for a short distance the Rhyd-ddu to Yr Wyddfa path, passing toilets on L. Later the path runs between houses (Tan yr Wyddfa), follow this down to main road. R along main road to Cwellyn Arms public house. **1.** L up road (B4418) and 10 metres after the 30mph sign R along forestry track. Follow this track which eventually narrows with rock wall on L and drop on R. At end of rock wall there is a clearing on L. Here half L up stone steps following edge of wood up to a stile. **2.** Over stile and R following fence on R and keep ascending, crossing two stiles and on to fence corner. Now up steep ridge later passing over low wall and up to saddle. Continue up ridge and onto to summit. **3.** From summit follow line of cairns (heading in the general direction of Afon Menai). Path soon runs close to the edge of the Cwm and passes small fenced mine working. **4.** On level ground at end of ridge a cairn of smelted copper marks the path. Continue on for 10 metres and half R along narrow path descending to a stream. Cross stream and half L up to wall corner and follow wall on R to cross another stream. **5.** Follow wall, on R passing kissing gate (this descends to the village of Betws Garmon and Bryn Gloch camping/caravan site). Continue following wall until a stile is reached. At stile continue straight on (leaving wall) along path in heather to the summit of Moel Smytho. **6.** From Moel Smytho summit follow descending path to enclosure. Follow wall on L and continue along track (do not take a L) to road. **7.** At road R descending over cattle grid and down to main road. L and along to the Snowdonia Parc hotel and Waunfawr station.

Refreshments: Pub grub is available at the Cwellyn Arms in Rhyd-ddu and at the Snowdonia Parc Hotel close to the station in Waunfawr. Afternoon teas at the Castell Cidwm hotel situated at the Waunfawr end of Llyn Cwellyn.

Garn Nantlle
and the Cwm Du Spur

Maps: 1:50,000 Landranger sheet 115 Yr Wyddfa *(Snowdon)* and Caernarfon or 1:25,000 Outdoor Leisure sheet 17 Yr Wyddfa *(Snowdon)* and Conwy.

Distance: 5 miles/8 kilometres.

Height gained: 1653ft/504 metres.

Duration: 4 hours.

Terrain: Good hard ground on clear paths. Some scrambling involved.

Station/Halts: Rhyd-ddu station.

Car Park: The pay and display car park at the Station in Rhyd-ddu. G.R.571525.

Garn Nantlle was once out of bounds to walkers. It is now, thanks to access agreements between the National Park Committee and the local farmers, open to the walking public. This access allows a traverse of the Nantlle ridge, often regarded as a walk second only to the Pedol yr Wyddfa *(Snowdon Horseshoe)*. This walk departs from the car park/station at Rhyd-ddu and crosses the busy A4085. Crossing the marshy area on a series of stepping-stones, the path crosses Afon Gwyrfai as it flows on its way from Llyn y Gadair to Llyn Cwellyn. At this point the remains of the intended branch line, which was to run from Rhyd-ddu to the Llyn y Gadair quarry, can be seen. Sadly this project was never completed.

Later at a large boulder indicating a path junction, a steep ascent is made up the flanks of Y Garn. As the upper fence is crossed look for an indentation in the ground, this is the remains of a leat that was constructed to collect water from the flanks of Y Garn and channel it to Llyn y Dywarchen. From here it was channelled to the hydraulic equipment being used in the mines. As the ascent is made, pause to view the spectacular westerly facing cwms of Yr Wyddfa and the remains of the Llyn y Gadair

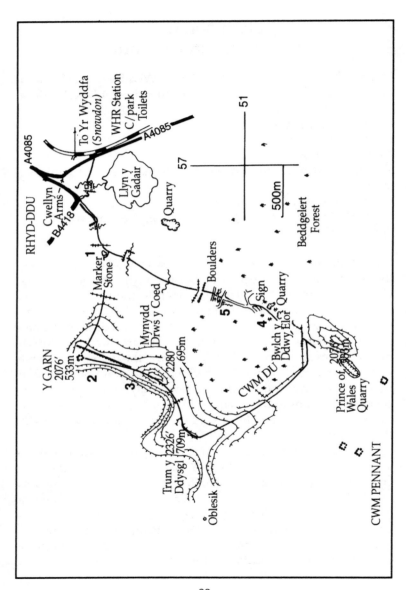

88

quarry. The glistening Llyn y Dywarchen, below Mynydd Mawr, was made famous by both Giraldus Cambrensis during his 12th century journeys through Wales and the Astronomer Edmond Halley in 1698. They both discovered that the lake had a floating island on its surface on which cattle used to graze; unfortunately the island is no longer there.

As the path levels out and draws near the summit, the dramatic cliffs of Craig y Bera on the flanks of Mynydd Mawr come into view. Below can be seen the remains of the Drws y Coed copper mines, thought at one time to have been the largest in Europe. Heavily mined between 1700 and the mid 1800's, they were owned during this period by the Assheton Smith family who also owned the Dinorwig slate quarries. The total output of these mines at Drws y Coed is thought to be in the region of 26,000 tons, but unfortunately the remaining records only indicate an extraction of some 13,000 tons. Extraction of ore from this area ceased in 1920.

From the summit of Y Garn, the Nantlle valley comes into view. This area was also one of the major slate producers in northern Wales, and because the valley floor was virtually solid Cambrian slate, most of the quarries were of the open pit type. One of the largest quarries was the famous Dorothea quarry. Now popular with sub-aqua enthusiasts craving the clarity of the water and challenging depth of the dives, which can descend the galleries to a total depth of 553 feet.

For the quarries in the Nantlle area the main problem was transportation of the final product to a port. Until 1828, the dressed slate was transported on horse back to the banks of the Foryd before being trans shipped to Caernarfon. Later on, horse drawn carts were used to transport the slate down the Nantlle valley to the port of Caernarfon. In the late 1800s, the L&NWR laid a standard gauge line from Afon Wen (between Criccieth and Pwhelli) to Caernarfon with a branch line from the village of Penygroes to the village of Tal-y-sarn. From here a 1.5 mile section from Tal-y-sarn to the Pen yr Orsedd quarry survived until 1963 as the only horse drawn line in existence owned by British Rail.

From the summit of Y Garn the ridgeline is an easy but exciting scramble. It gains the summit of Mynydd Drws y Coed and goes on to the summit of Trum y Ddysgl. Ahead can be seen the obelisk marking the summit of Mynydd Talymignedd, constructed by local quarry men to commemorate the jubilee of Queen Victoria. The obelisk, exposed to the elements since 1887 shows no signs of deterioration, a tribute to those craftsmen who constructed it. Sadly, it is not visited on this walk.

As the path descends the Cwm Du spur, the Cwm Pennant valley can be seen on the right with views as far as the sea in the Portmadog bay. In the distance can be seen the rocky outcrop of Moel y Gest. Cwm Pennant was the birthplace, and home, to the lyrical poet Eifion Wyn who wrote a special poem to his native cwm. One of its lines describes the poets feeling for the area, 'O God, why did'st thou make Cwm Pennant so beautiful and the life of an old shepherd so short?' He died at the age of 59 in 1926.

The path turns to pass through a gate and ascends to a pass, Bwlch y Ddwy Elor, *(pass of the two biers)* – a bier being a wooden framework with long carrying handles on which a body could be conveyed over a long distance to a graveyard. This signifies this route as a corpse road from Cwm Pennant, through Rhyd-ddu and on to reach the consecrated resting site at Llanberis. This was prior to the church in Cwm Pennant being both constructed and consecrated. The reason for two biers is unknown, perhaps one was lodged at the bwlch and the corpse was transferred from one to the other for its journey.

The path now descends into the forest passing the remains of the Bwlch y Ddwy Elor quarry and on to the forest roads running around the flanks of Mynydd Drws y Coed and Y Garn before returning to the Rhyd-ddu station and car park. Don't be alarmed if you are passed by Lycra clad bodies, some at high speed, on mountain bikes on the path from Bwlch y Ddwy Elor to Rhyd-ddu as this is a recognised mountain biking route from, and to Cwm Pennant.

The Walk: Depart from the car park and cross the main road to a kissing gate, through this and cross the marshy area on stepping stones to a stream. L upstream and R over bridge to follow arrowed footpath crossing lane to cottage. Later rejoin lane and over stile constructed from railway lines and up to road. At road L through gate and along path, with wall on R. Continue up to gate with stile, over stile and up to large boulder marked with white arrow. **1.** Up hill to fence, now over stile and continue up, path now zig zags up hill to summit plateau. From summit the path now crosses a boulder field to a wall with a stile. Cross this stile and continue up to the summit cairn. **2.** Return to the wall but do not cross it. Instead go R along wall, which is the lead in to the ridge, scramble up the ridge. For those who are not so adventurous there is a path a few meters lower down from the ridge. Continue along a now broader ridge to cross a fence. The path dips and then continues its ascent up to Mynydd Drws y Coed, again the easy scramble can be avoided by taking the lower path. **3.** From here on the ridge broadens, keep to the LH edge and where it starts to descend follow the initial steep drop around to the L and continue down the broad spur. The path now runs alongside a fence, continue down with fence on left. At a short wall with a gate go L through gate and follow path, which ascends at first then descends into the forest. The path now descends through the forestry, passing the remains of two quarries. **4.** At the junction with the forestry road (sign for Dolbenmaen), R to next junction. Here R down forestry road to sharp R/H bend, with stream and bridge on L. **5.** L over bridge and sharp R down to path passing between a row of large boulders and crossing a forestry road. The path passes through a wall gap and down to a fence with a gate and stile, through this and continue to a gully, pass over the stepping stones and on to the next gully. Through a gate, and pass a number of boulders with white arrows to indicate the path. Pass the junction for the ridge and descend the path back to the road. R over stile and along track. At R/H bend half L following arrows to stile and bridge over stream to return to car park and station.

NOTE. The return route from 4. is used by mountain bikers on their way to, and from Rhyd-ddu and Dolbenmaen.

Refreshments: The Cwellyn Arms in Rhyd-ddu is convenient and interesting. Beddgelert has plenty of choice to suit all tastes.

FURTHER READING

ERYRI The story of Snowdonia, Michel Senior.
Snowdonia, Jim Roberts.
Snowdon that most celebrated hill, Dennis Hoar.
Old Copper Mines in Snowdonia, David Bick.
Visions of Snowdonia, Jim Perrin
A regional history of the railways of Great Britain. Volume 2 North and Mid Wales, Peter E Baughan
Britains Light Railways, Martin Smith.
Rumours and Oddities from north Wales, Meirion Hughes & Wayne Evans.
Marconi and his wireless stations in Wales, Hari Williams.
Three stops to the summit. A history Of the Snowdon Mountain Railway, Rol Williams.
The Lakes of Eryri, Geraint Roberts.
Slate Quarrying in Wales, Alun John Richards
A Gazeteer of the Welsh Slate Industry, Alun John Richards

There are also a number of excellent web sites to the Welsh Highland Railway, notably www.bangor.ac.uk/ml/whr/.